Starfish

by **Trudi Strain Trueit**

Reading Consultant: Nanci R. Vargus, Ed.D.

Marshall Cavendish
Benchmark
New York

Picture Words

 bush

 candy cane

 cookie

 feathers

 flower

 spider

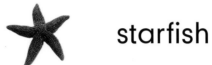 starfish

 starfish

 stars

 Sun

★★★ look like many things!

A  looks like a .

A  looks like a .

A  looks like the .

A looks like a .

A  looks like a .

A  looks like .

⭐⭐⭐ look like ⭐⭐⭐, too!

Words to Know

feathers (FETH-uhrs)
   the soft covering of birds

spider (SPY-duhr)
   a small animal with eight legs that
   spins webs

starfish (STAR-fish)
   a small sea animal that has five or
   more arms

Find Out More

Books

Clough, Julie. *The Starfish*. Hauppauge, NY: Barron's Educational Series, 2008.

Moss, Miriam. *This is the Reef*. London, England: Frances Lincoln Children's Books, 2008.

Pohl, Kathleen. *Animals of the Ocean*. Pleasantville, NY: Gareth Stevens, 2008.

DVD

Wondrous Secrets of the Ocean, Reader's Digest, 2007.

Websites

Monterey Bay Aquarium
www.mbayaq.org

National Geographic: Starfish
http://animals.nationalgeographic.com/animals/
invertebrates/starfish.html

Save Our Seas for Kids
www.saveourseas.com/minisites/kids/82.html

About the Author

Trudi Strain Trueit lives in Everett, WA, near Puget Sound, where she gets to see plenty of beautiful starfish. Trudi is the author of more than sixty fiction and nonfiction books for children, including *Sharks* and *Starfish* in the Benchmark Rebus Ocean Life series. She writes fiction, too, including the popular *Secrets of a Lab Rat* series. Visit her website at **www.trudistrueit.com.**

About the Reading Consultant

Nanci R. Vargus, Ed.D., wants all children to enjoy reading. She used to teach first grade. Now she works at the University of Indianapolis. Nanci helps young people become teachers. She enjoys vacationing on Cumberland Island, GA, where there are lots of starlike starfish.

This publication represents the opinions and views of the author based on Trudi Strain Trueit's personal experience, knowledge, and research. The information in this book serves as a general guide only. The author and publisher have used their best efforts in preparing this book and disclaim liability rising directly and indirectly from the use and application of this book.

Other Marshall Cavendish Offices:
Marshall Cavendish International (Asia) Private Limited, 1 New Industrial Road, Singapore 536196 • Marshall Cavendish International (Thailand) Co Ltd. 253 Asoke, 12th Flr, Sukhumvit 21 Road, Klongtoey Nua, Wattana, Bangkok 10110, Thailand • Marshall Cavendish (Malaysia) Sdn Bhd, Times Subang, Lot 46, Subang Hi-Tech Industrial Park, Batu Tiga, 40000 Shah Alam, Selangor Darul Ehsan, Malaysia

Marshall Cavendish is a trademark of Times Publishing Limited

All websites were available and accurate when this book was sent to press.

Library of Congress Cataloging-in-Publication Data

Trueit, Trudi Strain.
Starfish / Trudi Strain Trueit.
p. cm. — (Ocean life)
Includes bibliographical references.
Summary: "A simple introduction to starfish using rebuses"—Provided by publisher.
ISBN 978-0-7614-4894-5
1. Starfishes—Juvenile literature. I. Marshall Cavendish Benchmark. II. Title.
QL384.A8T78 2010
593.9'3—dc22
2009025475

Editor: Christina Gardeski
Publisher: Michelle Bisson
Art Director: Anahid Hamparian
Series Designer: Virginia Pope

Photo research by Connie Gardner
Cover photo by Chris Newbert/Minden Pictures

The photographs in this book are used by permission and through the courtesy of: *Minden Pictures*: pp. 5, 17 Norbert Wu; p. 7 Flip Nicklin, p. 13 Roblin Chittenden. *Getty Images*: p. 2 William J Hebert, bush, Photodisc, candy cane; Burzain, cookie; Niladri Nath, feathers; Martin Ruegner, flower; p. 3 Jerry Young, spider; Dorling Kindersley, Iconica, stars, sun; p. 9 Georgette Douwma, p. 11 Daniel Gatshall, p. 21 Connie Coleman. *Corbis*: p. 15 Hal Beral. *Photo Researchers*: p. 19 Georgette Douwma.

Printed in Malaysia (T)
1 3 5 6 4 2